MEMOIRS
OF OUR CABIN IN YOSEMITE;
AND OUR BACKYARD WILDERNESS

iUniverse, Inc.
New York Bloomington

Memoirs Of Our Cabin In Yosemite;
And Our Backyard Wilderness

iUniverse books may be ordered through booksellers or by contacting:

iUniverse
1663 Liberty Drive
Bloomington, IN 47403
www.iuniverse.com
1-800-Authors (1-800-288-4677)

ISBN: 978-1-4401-4080-8 (pbk)
ISBN: 978-1-4401-4082-2 (cloth)
ISBN: 978-1-4401-4081-5 (ebk)

Printed in the United States of America

iUniverse rev. date: 5/7/2009

MEMOIRS
OF OUR CABIN IN YOSEMITE;
AND OUR BACKYARD WILDERNESS

Sophia Kaeser

"A Remembrance of a time gone by;
    With no particular year and no specific age".......

Mark Vuletich

For My three Boys
Keith, Don and Mike
And their Families

What could be better than our family with three young boys spending time in and around Wawona, Yosemite where we built our little cabin? The series of events in our life there, as we reminisce about our cabin and our whole back yard of Yosemite.

I'd like to acknowledge a very special lady, Bonnie Sipe a Retired High School English Teacher, who took the time to edit my writings and to make sure that the punctuation marks were in the right place!

To my granddaughter Kayleen Donnelly who was there when I needed help with my computer.

And especially to my husband Keith, who encouraged and supported me with his love through it all.

DEDICATION

I would like to dedicate this book to our friends Andy and Virginia Marshall who started us on our wonderful journey into Yosemite. Andy is gone now, but Virginia and their family still have their little cabin.

To our late friends George and Dete Oliver who introduced us to Yosemite.

And to our friends Bill and Pat Krause that together we hiked around Yosemite. Bill is gone now, but Pat still lives in Wawona. And to our son's friend Steve Attardo who lives in Wawona, and to his late parents Frank and Lurlene who were fun to be with. And last, but least, to all our great friends from Yosemite!

Starting Out

My husband was discharged from military service in World II in 1945. We went camping in Yosemite for the first time in the summer of 1946 at the A. E. Wood campground in Wawona, (Wah-wo-nah, an Indian word meaning big trees,) The campground was named after Captain A. E. Wood, Commander of the Fourth Calvary and acting Superintendent of Yosemite National Park. His troop of men was bivouacked there in 1891.

On this first trip to Wawona, my husband and I were accompanied with another couple who were longtime friends and schoolmates of my husband. Our husbands were discharged from the service around the same time, and were anxious to go camping in Yosemite.

Each of us left our children home this time. Our family consisted of my husband, me, and three boys: Keith, Donald, and Michael. Our friends had a boy and a girl around the same ages as our boys; they later had another boy.

Looking for Property

After several years of camping together, our families decided to look for property to buy. We loved the area, and being in the mountain wilderness. We thought it would be great to have something of our own to come to instead of camping.

While we were in a little café and grocery store in Wawona, we asked the proprietors if they knew of any lots for sale. They said there were some, and told us where they were. The lots were located two or three miles off the main highway in Wawona. Off that road, and down a rutted, dirt road surrounded by many tall sugar pines and cedar, dense brush and dead trees, were the lots we were looking for. There were six lots in all, and some people were starting to build on two of them. Across the dirt road from the lot we liked was an old empty cabin. The lot our friends and my husband and I decided to buy was about forty-five yards from the cliff.

Down below, about a hundred feet, was the south fork of the Merced River, called the Chilanualna River in Wawona. The lot cost one thousand dollars! That was a lot of money in those days. We didn't have our half of five hundred dollars at the time. However, our good friends did, and paid the full amount. We agreed to pay a sum of money every month until the loan was paid.

Cabin Construction Begins

Before we divided the property in half, we had to clear it of all the dense brush and dead trees before we could start building. We appreciated the fact that we didn't have to cut down any trees to start building. We divided the property and started one cabin. My husband borrowed his father's big truck to haul all the lumber up that he bargained for at the lumberyard. He also bartered for the other things we would need. It all worked out so that we had new and used materials in building our little cabins.

We all stayed in the first cabin; it was not finished but livable. Our family slept in the loft area and their family slept downstairs. At the time we bought the lot, Keith was twelve, Don was nine, and Mike was seven. . Again with the help of our friends, their children, and our boys, we started the second cabin.

With the second cabin progressing, we agreed that my friend and I would cut cards to see which cabin we'd get. One day while we took a much needed break from helping with the building, we decided this was a good time to cut the cards.

The first cabin built would be a low card; it was lower on our slanted property. The second cabin would be a high card as it was built on a little higher ground. As it turned out, I chose a high card, and our friend got a low card. We were each pleased with our choices. As we liked either cabins. It didn't make any difference which one we picked. We then proceeded to finish our own cabins with the help of our children.

Finishing our own Cabin

Our cabin had a very high pitched A-frame roof. When putting on the roofing material, my husband tied a rope around my waist and held on to my legs. I hammered the nails onto the high roof while lying on my stomach. It was definitely a family project!

As our family came up more often, our little cabin was ready to move into. It still had a lot of work to do inside, but we were able to live in it. Our cabin had one large room and a loft where the boys slept. Later, my husband added a bedroom for us, and then a kitchen and bathroom. He was, as the old saying goes, "A Jack of all trades."

Sharing with Bears

In the early years, we had an outhouse. Our trips to the outhouse were sometimes adventurous and scary, because at times we met up with bears making their way to and from the river.

While building our cabin, we had many experiences with bears trying to get into our ice-chest. We kept it outside where it was cool and where food was stored. In addition to bears, we would also see deer, raccoons, and coyotes.

One day the Ranger came by to see how we were getting along with our little cabin. He told us that we had built our cabin on an animal path and they seldom changed their route. That explained why we saw an abundance of wildlife. We couldn't imagine building anywhere else. We liked our location and enjoyed seeing all of the animal wildlife. Besides, there was nothing we could do about it now.

A Great Privilege

All the people who owned cabins in Wawona were issued passes. We were given a sticker to place in the corner of our windshield. That would get us through the gate to Yosemite National Park. There was a ranger on duty at each entrance. Ours was the south entrance coming from Fresno. To us, it was a great privilege and pleasure to come through the gate into Yosemite.

There was a place on the road leaving Fish Camp, and before getting to the entrance gate, that all the college kids working in Yosemite would honk their horns twice passing this certain area. We never knew why they did, but our boys wanted us to do the same. So every time we'd pass that area, we'd honk our horn twice!

Same Every Year

Cabin Fever was what we had! Only ours was the kind that meant we could hardly wait to be at our little cabin. We went up on all weekends, all holidays, and school vacations. Our boys spent their childhood in and around the backyard wilderness of Yosemite National Park. It began much the same every year!

School for our boys was over and it was summer again. Our family eagerly awaited departure from our home in Monterey Park to the little cabin. I drove our son Don up in our old truck, and our sons Keith, and Mike rode up with their Dad. That way we would have the truck in the mountains, and my husband could come up every weekend.

Don and I started out early in the morning as it took seven to eight hours to get there. The old ridge route was a winding two-lane road through the mountains towards Bakersfield. It turned out to be a very hot day. Our truck started to overheat and I began to feel the heat. It was over one hundred degrees and there was no air-conditioning in our old truck.

We had to make several stops to cool the truck. One of the stops after we left the ridge route was in an orchard with a lot of trees. There we could sit in the shade, and cool the truck and ourselves, and rest a bit. Don had other ideas. He was climbing the trees.

The heat never seemed to bother him at all. I couldn't believe all his energy in that heat. He kept asking me if he could drive as I was not feeling that good. Don had his learners permit waiting for his driver's license in the mail, and could drive with an adult.

I finally let him drive, and on our way we went towards the mountains. I had brought along a big round thermos jug. We had cool water to drink and water to cool down our faces. We kept that up until we got to Fresno.

Just on the side of the road was a big sign saying, *all the lemonade you can drink for ten cents.* We stopped and drank a couple of glasses. There, we met a golfing friend who was on her way to the mountains, too. She saw what shape I was in and invited me to drive the rest of the way with her in her air-conditioned car. I politely thanked her, and said I wouldn't leave my son. He was so good about driving us and really enjoyed doing it.

Almost Company for Dinner

When we all finally arrived at our cabin, it was so good to be in the cool mountain air with the sweet-smelling, beautiful pine trees. We were thrilled to see our little cabin just waiting for us to unpack and move in! It was exciting for Keith, Don and Mike to be there after being in school all that time. After we unpacked, I fixed dinner and since it was such a beautiful evening I decided we would eat out on the deck.

After dinner, while our sons helped clear the table, we saw a mother bear and her two cubs running down the dirt road in front of our cabin. We wondered why they were in a hurry. We soon saw why! Coming down the road was a huge male bear chasing them. The mother bear helped her cubs climb up a tree and she stood right there to protect them from the male bear.

We didn't know whether we should go inside the cabin and watch out our windows, or stay where we were on the deck. We just figured if they looked our way we would all run inside the cabin. The bears were so engrossed in what they were doing, that they didn't even look over at us watching them. Therefore, we stayed where we were. The male bear circled the tree several times trying to get to the cubs, but the mother bear was not about to let him.

She kept in front of him, protecting her cubs so that he could not climb the tree. He finally gave up and went on his way down to the river. The mother bear and her cubs went in the other direction. The Ranger had warned us that we would see many animals go by, and we sure did!

Enjoying the Golf Course

It was getting late and Keith, Don and Mike were tired from the long drive and unpacking. As they went up to the loft to get ready for bed, we heard Keith say "It's sure good to be up here in the mountains again." And Don replied "Yes, it's like our whole backyard." Moreover, my husband and I thought the same. The boys spent most of their youth here.

The boys planned to work again on the golf course as caddies. The Pro had given the boys lessons when they first started caddying. Watching the golfers they had picked it up quickly. What they learned, they showed my husband and me, and we also took some lessons. The Pro said our sons taught us well.

I belonged to the women's golf club in Wawona. When I was in a golf tournament, the boys would surprise me by sitting on an embankment on the third hole amongst the pine trees, rooting for me. I could hear them encouraging me on. The other women would get a kick out of it saying, "You have your own cheering section."

Finding the Fawn

Whenever the boys were through caddying for the day, they would go out on the course to play golf after dinner. Though it was still light enough to play, there were very few golfers out at that time of evening.

On one of the evenings, while playing golf, the boys came across a baby fawn lying in the rough, all cuddled up and whimpering. They thought it was crying because it was all alone. Its mother was nowhere around. However, the boys didn't want to touch the fawn in case she was. They went on their way thinking that the mother would be back.

The next evening they played golf again and looked for the little fawn, all they saw was the imprint where it had lain. They assumed that the mother had returned and taken the fawn. The next day, the boys learned that someone in our little community had rescued the fawn, figuring that the mother had been killed by a coyote while defending her baby.

The fawn evidently had been alone for a few days and was hungry. Several families in Wawona banded together and shared in raising the little male deer. We named him *"Bambi"* after the Disney character. He became so tame and friendly that he would approach everyone for a loving pat or a treat. He grew up fast with all the loving care.

Mike gets a new job

Keith and Don were very good caddies and many golfers would always ask for them, but Mike didn't care that much for caddying.

The manager of the Wawona hotel saw Mike on a huge airplane inner tube that his Dad brought up for him. Mike would straddle it like riding a horse, with a rope around it to hold on to, with his feet on the inside. Mike jumped all around the lawn in front of the Hotel and Golf Shop. Several caddies tried to ride, but didn't have the balance they needed to stay on. Mike didn't have any trouble staying on.

The manager asked the Pro, "Who's that redhead on the inner tube?" The Pro said, "Why that's Mike, the youngest of the three brothers." Well, the manager said, "I've heard he's the worst caddy!" The Pro then told him that, when the Governor of our state came up on vacation, he always asked for Mike to caddy. Mike wasn't enjoying it any more. So the last time he caddied for the Governor, he told him he was going to quit, and look for a job cleaning cabins.

Mike thought he would like that much better. When the Governor came in carrying his own bag, Keith and Don where puzzled and wondered what happened to Mike. The Governor told them that Mike just didn't care to caddy anymore and he didn't mind carrying his own bag back to the clubhouse.

Keith and Don told their brother he should let the Pro know that he had decided to look for another job, and Mike did. The Pro told him to "Go for it!"

Mike then went to the owners of some rental cabins and asked if they needed help in cleaning their cabins. They said yes, and also hired him to drive a little truck, taking the trash to the dump. Mike was doing what he liked and Keith and Don were doing what they liked. So the boys were happy.

Don becomes a Cook

While Keith and Don were in the golf shop waiting to caddy, someone came in from the Wawona Hotel, and told them that the second cook was ill, and they needed to replace him quickly. Did they know of anyone who could cook a little? Don thought a moment, and decided to try for the job. Occasionally, he liked cooking a few things for himself.

It would be something different, so he volunteered and went up to the Hotel with the young man. Don was shown the big kitchen, and told what his duties were. When Keith came back to the cabin and told me about Don, I couldn't believe it. I told Keith, "I know I taught you boys how to cook some things, but I can't believe he would volunteer for the Hotel." As it turned out, he did very well. When the second cook recovered after a week, and returned to work, Don went back to the golf course to caddy.

One of Don's frequent golfers for whom he caddied told him of a dream she had the night before. In the dream, Don was making pancakes, and in flipping them, they had all stuck to the ceiling. He and the caddies thought it was pretty funny!

Going Fishing

One day, Keith and Don decided to take a day off to go fishing. They asked the Pro if they could have the next day off. He said, "Its fine with me. I wished I could go with you." Mike also asked for the day off so he could go, too.

After breakfast that morning, the boys were out on the deck getting their fishing gear together when a shadow came across the deck. They looked up and saw a huge eagle swoop down to pick up a ground squirrel. Even if they hadn't seen this, they would have heard the squealing, it was so loud. They felt sorry for the poor ground squirrel. When we went to the edge of our cliff, we'd occasionally see an eagle fly by. However we had never seen one this close to the cabin before. It was quite a sight.

The boys decided to hike up to Chilanualna Falls that morning, on a switch back trail all the way up to the falls. It was a long hike. The start of the trail was approximately a hundred yards from our cabin. I packed them a good lunch for their backpack. Off they went up the trail, taking turns carrying the backpack which also contained their fishing gear. They each carried their own fishing poles.

A Close Encounter

Halfway up the trail they saw a huge bear lumbering down the path towards them. Keith yelled, "Quick, run up the side!" They ran off the main path and hid behind a big pine tree and some shrubbery, hoping that the bear wouldn't notice them. As they stood there, they wondered what they would do if the bear looked up and saw them hiding or smelled their food. They were pretty scared thinking about it. As it turned out, the bear was in a hurry and didn't look their way as he ran down the path. The boys looked at each other and realized they'd each been holding their breath. They were glad that the bear didn't notice them and just went on his way. They still waited a while to make sure he was far enough away from them before finally going on to their fishing hole. They hoped they wouldn't come across any more bears!

When they arrived at the spot, Keith baited their hooks as Don and Mike didn't like touching the worms. Both boys caught fish right away, and again, Keith baited their hooks. When Keith started to bait his own hook, they'd catch fish again!

Every time he would begin to bait his hook, Mike and Don would reel in fish and ask their brother to take the fish off their hooks and bait them. He did it again, but said, "Hey, you two, you can bait your own hooks and take your own fish off from now on. I haven't even put my pole in yet and I want to catch some fish, too."

By the time they caught their limit, it had gotten quite late, and it was a long hike back. Luckily, the way home was mostly downhill. They didn't encounter any bears on the way back, and were thankful for that. However, they did see something disturbing. They watched a bushy grey squirrel run up a pine tree to a blue jay's nest and get to all the babies. They understood that was the way of nature in the woods, but they didn't like seeing it.

I had become a little worried because they had never been so late before. As I headed for our truck to ask the Ranger for help, they strolled in, tired but satisfied. Mike said, "I told them to come home sooner, but they wouldn't listen to me." Keith and Don said "We were having such a good time catching fish; we didn't want to leave until all of us caught our limit.

Our Animal Visitors

When their Dad came up that evening we had a delicious fish dinner that he barbequed out on the deck. After our dinner this time, two raccoons and a deer wandered by. The deer wasn't our *Bambi*; it was a female deer and she was a little skittish. I guess they had smelled our fish.

We all hoped that no bears would come by while we were eating out there. We left a little fish for the raccoons to enjoy. We heard a noise after we had been inside awhile. Looking out the window, we saw a mother bear and her two cubs nosing around. We figured they also smelled our fish but there wasn't any left after the raccoons got through. We were so glad we were inside our cabin and glad when the bears left!

We still had our bears visit us occasionally at night trying to get some food, but we now had a refrigerator and didn't have to leave our ice chest outside any more. My husband had fixed a heavy screen on the kitchen window so we didn't have any more bears climbing in that way. It was funny to watch them still try to get in. Occasionally we saw them trying to get hold of the screen, but this time the screen wouldn't budge. Frustrated, they would finally give up and go on their way, probably wondering why the screen didn't come off when other times it had been so easy!

We still kept the greasy paw print that a bear once left on our wall in the kitchen. The boys didn't want me to wash it off. It was a reminder of when the bear sat at our table, and cleaned out the jars of peanut butter and jelly. The boys had left the jars on the table when they were in a hurry to get back to work.

Whenever we heard noises in the yard or on our deck, we'd look out the window. Sure enough, it would be a bear or two nosing around our cabin, sometimes looking in the windows. Not bothering them, we just enjoyed looking out at them looking in at us.

Strange Neighbors

Across the road from our cabin was the older cabin that had been empty when we first bought our lot. It was now occupied with new owners, who came up once in a while. Although we didn't know them very well, we thought they were a little eccentric, for they owned fifty cats. The woman drove a good-size motor home just for their fifty cats to ride up in. The husband drove up in his car.

One day as I came down the main road back from playing golf, I met the neighbor. She was leaving in her motor home with all her cats. She stopped on the road to say goodbye, and I wished her a safe journey. As she drove away, I noticed an open window with no screen in the motor home. The cats were moving all around. We just couldn't get over how many she had!

That night around midnight, our phone rang and awakened us. As my husband was down in the city working, getting a phone call in the middle of the night was a bit frightening. I answered it, and it was the neighbor from across the road. She asked me to go outside and look for one of her cats. "One of them is missing!" she said. I told her, "Its twelve o' clock at night, and pitch- black outside." "I'll go looking in the morning." She hung up, and we all tried to go back to sleep.

The next morning we looked all around our mutual places, but didn't see or hear a cat. However, on their way to work, the boys saw all this commotion down on the main road. It was her cat high up in a huge pine tree, crying. The power company had to come up with their big crane to get the cat down. The neighbor returned early that morning and got her cat. We didn't see much of them, and once in a while we'd see a cat or two. It's a wonder the coyotes or bears didn't get them. I guess she kept them mostly in her cabin or their motor home. Wow, 50 cats!

Holiday at our cabin

We came up to our little cabin on all holidays, especially Christmas Vacation.

It often snowed quite a bit, and when we came to the dirt road above our cabin, there was usually deep snow on the ground. Although the main roads were plowed, our road was not, so we couldn't drive down to our cabin.

We didn't have four-wheel drive, and even if we had, the snow was so deep we couldn't drive down to the cabin.

Don waded down with snow past his knees, to get the toboggan stored in the shed. We put our groceries and belongings on the toboggan, and pulled it down to the cabin. The boys also had a lot of fun sliding down the hill on the toboggan during our snowy visits.

The snow on the young pine tree at the entrance to our driveway was bent over with snow, making an archway across the driveway. It looked as if it was purposely put there. It looked so good that we left it that way. The boys put a sign with our name on it, and being boys, put a hangman's knot on it.

They thought it would look good up there too! My husband and I laughed about it and told them they could keep it that way.

A Power Outage

On this visit the snow came down all night. It was really quiet, and we could actually hear the snow falling. We woke up to a bone-chilling cold cabin. We had no power, so we quickly made a fire in the fireplace and I made oatmeal for breakfast over the fire. It turned out pretty good and warmed us up. Then my husband decided to go out to patrol the lines. He went to the shed to put on his snowshoes, picked up a sledge hammer, and went to find the outage. Since he worked for a major power company in the city, he knew all about power lines.

He found a tree branch heavy with snow lying across the line. He hit the bottom of the tree several times with the sledge hammer. The vibration knocked the snow off the branch, and it rose up off the power line. As he walked back, he met the power crew, and told them what he had done. They thanked him, and called in to have the circuit checked. The power came back on.

We then heated the cabin, and before long it was nice and cozy, and warm. We had to be careful to heat our cabin up slowly when we first arrived in the winter, so the pipes wouldn't burst. They were wrapped, but sometimes that didn't help.

Water Everywhere

On one Christmas vacation Mike and I went up a day ahead of his Dad and brothers. We put our electric heater on high as soon as we got in, not knowing about slowly heating the cabin. We unpacked and went to dinner at the hotel.

While we were gone, the pipes burst. There was water all over the kitchen and the living room when we got back. I was so upset! How were we going to get all that water out of our cabin? With quick thinking, Mike took the baseboards off and drilled holes in the wall by the floor. Water began to drain out and we mopped up the rest.

Mopping up took most of the night. We rolled up the carpet and put it out on the deck, forgetting that it would freeze as it was soaking wet. It froze solid! A good friend tied it on top of his small Volkswagen the next day. He took it to Fresno, to have it dried and cleaned. He didn't realize it would thaw out as he was driving down.

As the carpet thawed, it drooped in front of his windshield and down the back window. He could hardly see out the front or the back. It looked very funny as he was driving with this big, limp roll of carpet on top of his small car. We got the carpet back in a few days and it was as good as new. When my husband arrived, he fixed the holes that Mike had drilled.

Tree Hunting

We always decorated our cabin for the holidays. Mike and I went walking in the snow by the river bed looking for a tree to cut down with the small saw blade Mike put inside his jacket. We spotted what we thought was a perfect tree on the other side of the river. We had to cross the river on a tree that had fallen across. As the tree was covered with snow, we had to step sideways, very cautiously.

The pine tree looked like a perfect Christmas tree, so standing on a nearby stump, and reaching high, Mike sawed off about five feet of the top, figuring the tree would grow a new top. As he was carrying it back up to the cabin, we heard some voices from one of the cabins above. Mike quickly stuck the tree in the snow, so it would look as if it were growing there. We laughed as we went back; carrying the tree to the cabin and hoping no one had seen us. I later found out that the community provided trees for all cabin owners, so no one would be tempted to cut down the trees! I felt terrible, and told Mike we wouldn't do that again, though it was fun getting our own tree. The cabin looked very festive and smelled like Christmas!

Skiing on the Slopes

Keith, Don and Mike, and my husband and I had two weeks to ski at the Badger Pass Ski Slopes. We all took a few lessons with a ski instructor, a friend who lived in Wawona. He came from Montreal, Canada, and had a slight accent. Sometimes when the ski instructor rode up with us, there would be four of us in the front seat. We all seemed to get car sick going around the curves to the ski slopes. When we'd be skiing anywhere near him, he would call out, "*Benz zee Knees.*" So we always did what he said!

The boys entered ski races, and were, surprisingly, very good. Their names are engraved, along with other skier's names, on wooden skis in the cafeteria where visitors can see their names to this day. Every winter would find our family skiing at Badger Pass, enjoying every exhilarating run!

During the Christmas holidays, the Ahwahnee Hotel down in the valley put on a Christmas Pageant. Held every year since 1927, it's called "The Bracebridge Dinner." The dining hall completely changed into a 17th century English Manor.

Guests are served a seven-course dinner, with formal dress required. Our family attended this ceremony a few times, and thoroughly enjoyed the four-hour pageant each time.

Spring Snow

Back at the cabin our sons saw a little deer and wondered if it was our *Bambi* because he came right up to them. His antlers were starting to show, and he was close to becoming a full-grown buck. The boys talked to him and he acted as if he knew what they were saying. He stayed around for a while probably hoping for something to eat. My sons and I didn't think we should feed him because he was undomesticated now and on his own. When we did not give him anything, he finally went on his way down towards the river.

When we came up on Easter vacation, there was still snow on the ground. This time there wasn't a bear hibernating under the cabin like another time, when their Dad was installing a dryer.

He had asked Mike to go through the crawl hole, as it was too small for him, , but told Mike what to do. The boys had learned a lot about wiring while building our cabin. Unknown to the both of them, a bear was hibernating under there, too. When we saw the bear come out the next day, we were shocked and amazed that Mike had been under there with him and nothing happened. We figured he was sleeping, and didn't see or hear Mike. However, when the bear finally woke up that next day and saw there was still snow on the ground, he scooted back under.

My husband and I had heard little noises from under the floor of our bedroom, and wondered at the time what it was! When we finally knew it was a bear, we called the Ranger who tranquilized him with a dart, then pulled him out. After that, my husband fixed another heavy screen for the crawl hole.

Our family spent the days skiing most of the winter, and some of spring. We were quite good now, and really took a lot of pleasure and enjoyment in it. When we came back from skiing all day, we'd have a nice dinner and afterwards sit around our cozy fireplace, and talk about what a wonderful day we had on the slopes. We heard a little noise outside the bay window, and there looking at us, were two little raccoons in the pine trees that my husband built our deck around. They looked so cute and stayed awhile and then left.

Keith, the Assistant Pro

Vacation was almost over and we were getting ready to leave for our home in the city. Keith, almost eighteen now, was asked by the Pro to become his assistant in the summer. He would give a few lessons. Keith was a three handicap at the time which is very good in golf. (Pros do not have a handicap; they're called scratch golfers.) Keith was excited and a little apprehensive and could hardly wait for summer.

When school let out for summer vacation again, Keith, Don and Mike eagerly awaited to leave for our little cabin in Wawona. This was the time Keith was going to become an assistant to the Pro. He was anxious to start giving lessons, and had confidence in his teaching ability.

After all, the Pro thought he was capable; that's why he made him his assistant. He gave a few lessons, and thought the sign inside the Pro Shop which said "Lessons: such, and such amount" applied to him. Nevertheless, he found out from the Pro that he was supposed to get only half of what the sign said. After all, he was just his assistant!

Some Influential Golfers

Keith and Don also continued to caddy, often for some influential golfers from the Bay area. One was a four-star General that Keith caddied for and Don caddied for the Dean of a big University. One elderly couple in particular, that owned a well-known lumber company in the Bay area, were favorites of Don and Keith. In fact, she was the one who had that dream of Don tossing the pancakes that stuck to the ceiling.

They traveled to Yosemite every summer and stayed at the Wawona Hotel for a month. Because they were such an interesting couple, Don and Keith were happy to be invited for dinner at their hotel.

I also invited them down to our cabin for dinner. On these occasions, they hoped to see some bears visiting as they had heard so much about them from Keith and Don. Much to their disappointment, no bears appeared during these visits. Our boys were very impressed with them as they were a lovely old couple.

Hanging Out with the Big Boys

On most evenings after dinner, the boys would ask if they could return to the golf course to help the greens keeper water the course. They helped him carry the long hoses around to water the course. He was a college student working during summer, and they liked him a lot.

On weekends, a few of the college students, working in Wawona, would come by and ask my husband and me if it were all right to take Keith, Don and Mike to the Lodge at Fish Camp. They promised they would watch over them.

These students were polite and trustworthy, so we felt the boys were in good hands. We also knew the owners of the lodge, and knew they would be fine. The boys watched the college student's dance and have fun and wished they knew how to dance.

The summer workers were carefully chosen. Each year, they selected students from different states and colleges. That summer, the students were from Tennessee and had a different way of dancing the swing dance, *jitterbug;* it was fun to watch them. They were all having such a good time. Don, Keith and Mike wished they could join in, but figured they had to learn how to dance first.

Dance Lessons

The next day, the boys asked me to teach them how to dance. I was quite surprised, but told them I would when they came home that afternoon. They were anxious to start right away when they got back to the cabin.

We rolled up the rug, moved some furniture out of the way, and put on some music. Keith, Don, and Mike took turns with me, and it was really fun. We laughed a lot, as they stepped all over my toes. I told them they had two left feet, but their enthusiasm was overwhelming!

With a few afternoons of practice, they finally had the confidence to ask the girls to dance. The next time they went with their friends to the Lodge, they had a good time.

A Visiting Cousin

In the meantime, Keith and Don went back to their jobs at the golf course and Mike went back to cleaning cabins. The boys, cousin, Barbara, came up to stay part of the summer. Mike and Barbara were the same age and grew up together. Her mother was my sister.

Mike asked the owner if Barbara could help clean the cabins with him, and received permission. One day they were feeling lazy, but were supposed to clean and make up two beds in one of the cabins. Instead, they each flopped down lying on the beds, talking about where they would go swimming when they got through with all the cabins.

The owner walked in and saw them lying down on the job and said, "You're wasting a lot of time, and it will just take you longer to finish." They told him, "We were just taking a quick break." He laughed at them as he left.

One day as they walked to work, they came across a porcupine waddling along and Mike decided to help him along. With a long branch, he guided him into a phone booth. He closed the door thinking to surprise someone when they came to make a phone call. Of course his cousin, and his conscience, got the best of him so he released the porcupine. It's a wonder he didn't shoot his quills at Mike!

While Barbara stayed with us, the boys introduced her to their friends, and took her swimming, hiking, and to Fish Camp. They had a lot of fun, but then it was finally time for her to leave and get ready for school.

A trip into Yosemite Valley

After the boys were through working for the day, they asked if we could go down to the valley to see a movie. The theater was in an old building that was used for something else during the day.

I thought it was a good idea, and said they could sit in the back of the truck bed. (That was before it was against the law.) The brothers fixed it with their sleeping bags and blankets so it would be soft for them to sit in the back.

On the way to the valley, we saw a coyote running along the side of the road. I slowed down, thinking they'd like to see the coyote up close, not knowing that the coyote was about to climb into the back of the truck. They yelled at me to keep going, I finally realized what was happening and drove away in a hurry.

After the show, we went to a little cafeteria for some ice cream where Keith, Don and I ordered ice cream. Mike hesitated, and then told us he was ordering a salad! We couldn't believe he was ordering that instead of ice cream. We thought it was odd, but that's what he wanted. To this day, he still likes salads!

Instead of going back to Wawona right away, I drove over to a good lookout spot to watch the fire falls. That was an awesome sight which we never got tired of watching. On our way back to the cabin, the boys enjoyed looking up at the stars as they lay in the back of the truck. They thought it was really neat to make a wish each time they saw a falling star. By the time we finally reached the cabin, they were sound asleep.

Television Arrives in Wawona

We finally got television in our little community. A friend, an executive for the Curry Co., and my husband put a transmitter on a high mountain peak so everyone would get good reception. He asked the boys and their friend to dig a trench for the underground cable, which they did on their days off. We had to buy an antenna to get the three main channels, but could not put it on our steep, pitched roof.

One day, the boys tried to find a good spot from which we could get the best reception. I stayed inside watching our small TV while they moved the antenna around outside. They finally got tired moving it and leaned it against our truck when they heard me call out, "The picture is perfect, leave it where it is!"

Not realizing it was just up against the truck, I came out to see. We all started laughing, wondering how we could solve this problem. Finally we decided to leave it where it was. So every time the truck was parked in front of the cabin, the antenna went into a slot on the inside of the truck bed and we had great reception.

The Television Takes Off

One day Keith and Don were in a hurry to get to work, and jumped in the truck and backed out of our yard, forgetting that the antenna was still on the back of the truck bed.

I was in the kitchen when they drove off. I heard a noise in the living room, and then saw the TV sliding across the room where it had fallen off its stand. I yelled at the boys to stop the truck. They didn't hear me at first, so I kept yelling. Finally, they heard me.

When I showed them that the TV had almost made it out the front door, they couldn't believe it. However it didn't hurt it at all, which was unbelievable! After that, we always made sure we took the antenna out of the truck before we drove off!

One of Many Swimming Holes

Keith, Don, and Mike loved to go swimming every chance they got. For a few years, we had a swimming hole just below our cabin, but one winter a big flood diverted the water and left it high and dry. After that, everyone's favorite swimming hole became the Chilanualna River, the south fork of the Merced River across from the ninth hole.

As it was so close to the golf course, the swimming hole could be conveniently reached by crossing the main road and the Wawona Bridge.

There, surrounded by many different-sized boulders, was a lovely sandy beach. From one of the huge granite boulders, the boys could dive or jump into the river and swim for many happy hours.

One day, a buck with full-grown antlers strolled up and sat down with the boys on their beach towels. They were certain it was *Bambi* because he showed no fear of them and seemed to listen as they talked to him. When the boys went back into the water, *Bambi* sat on their towels for quite awhile, just watching them swim and dive. Then he got up and walked away down along the river.

Bambi also returned and sat by us ladies when we went for a swim after playing golf. We were always happy and excited when he visited us.

Goodies, a Show and A Frightening Sight

After work one day the boys had planned to go to Bass Lake with Don driving and Keith in front with him. The other two caddies and Mike rode in the back. Bass Lake had a small old theater made out of logs and a *Bakery!* Leaving around four that afternoon, they hit the *Bakery* as soon as they arrived.

They all went in and bought pastries, except for one boy who bought a loaf of bread. The boys thought it was odd and Don asked him, "Why a loaf of bread, when there are so many desserts to pick from?" He said, "That's what I like," and Don told him about Mike and his choice of salad instead of ice cream.

They went inside the theater to watch the picture, eating their choice of goodies, and the one caddy eating his loaf of bread!

Keith drove on the return trip with Don up front with him. They made the usual arrangements as before with sleeping bags and blankets in the back of the truck.

On their way to Wawona, they saw an awesome and scary sight. A huge cougar with a long tail began to run along the side of the road right next to the truck. The boys in the back sat up to look, but immediately lay back down so he wouldn't see them.

The cougar ran ahead and leaped right in front of Keith and Don over the front of truck to the other side, then disappeared into the woods. The cougar could have jumped right in the back of the truck. It was scary to see this big animal which you don't anticipate being out there. Thank goodness, the rest of the ride to Wawona was uneventful. What a relief!

A Devastating Fire

Our cabin was near what we called our point, where there was a big drop off down to the river. Across our point was the Wawona Dome, and far up in the distance, was Wawona Point.

When there was a summer thunder storm, we'd go out on our point to watch the lightning and hear the thunder. It was something to see the lightning hitting the trees in the distance below Wawona Point, and some catching on fire. It was devastating to see the trees burst into flame and be consumed. Pretty soon the helicopter would come and dump water on the fire, and eventually would extinguish it..

A Great Fishing Trip

There was a path behind our cabin that was below the Wawona Dome and about a mile to the swinging bridge. This bridge was suspended by cables and its wooden walk way would sway as we walked on it. Another great swimming hole was there. The other one where the boys also liked to fish and swim was up by Chilanualna Falls. They could take these different hikes to swim or fish or both on their days off.

Keith and his friend, the Ranger's son, decided to go on an overnight fishing trip to Ostrander Lake. They left after an early dinner, and drove up to Glacier Point, and parked their car, and started to hike. It was five o'clock in the evening, with a six or seven mile hike to the Ostrander Ski Hut, where they had planned to stay.

The only drawback was that the Ski Hut was closed in the summer months, and open only during winter. But they planned to climb up and sleep on the balcony in their sleeping bags (with their food) in case of any bear activity.

His friend had brought a snack of boiled potatoes with butter, salt and pepper which they ate on the way up. I packed a couple of cans of beans, some fruit, nuts and homemade cookies for them.

They got there around nine o'clock that evening. The next morning they made a little fire to heat their cans of beans and had some fruit. That was their breakfast. They squashed the cans and put them back in their backpack, then doused the fire, and cleaned up around their area and went by the lake to fish.

The fishing wasn't good at all, so they decided to hike to the smaller Heart Lake, about a half a mile. There was no trail, and they had to hike through dense brush. Keith caught a 21 inch rainbow trout, but didn't have a net to bring him in, so they had to scoop it up with their hands.

Again they made a little fire, and cooked their fish for lunch, and ate some fruit, nuts and cookies. It was a lunch they really enjoyed. They cleaned up before leaving the area. When Keith came back to the cabin, he told us what a great time he had.

How did it get in?

Keith and Don came down to the cabin late one afternoon to fix themselves some lunch and got a surprise as they entered. Flying around inside the cabin was a bat! They ran outside and wondered what to do. How would they get it outside, and how did the bat get inside in the first place?

The bat made quite a mess, knocking things over. They finally managed to get the broom, however they were scared the bat would get in their hair. They had heard somewhere that bats do that. They tried to chase it out our front door or the kitchen door.

After several tries they finally chased it out, but we never did find out how it got inside. The boys had a lot of cleaning and straightening up to do before I came back from playing golf.

It reminded them of another time when they returned and entered the cabin through the front door and immediately fell on the couch, tired from a long hike. They heard a noise, looked up, and saw a bear crawling through the kitchen window. When the bear saw them, he hightailed it right back out. We had many encounters with bears in and around our cabin.

Picnics and Parties

Twice a month our golf group would have pot-luck picnics after a golf tournament. We also had cocktail parties and dinner parties. It was surprising how many people we could get in our little cabin. It was a fun group.

At a few of my dinner parties a friend, who was a priest, liked to come and help me in the kitchen.

The Catholic Church bought a cabin as a retreat for the priests. They also held services on Sunday at the *Hill Studio,* next to the Wawona Hotel. Their retreat was across the river from us, and across the road from our friend's cabin, who were the parents of our son's friend.

These same parents would ride with us in our truck whenever we went to a cocktail or dinner party down in the Valley. She and I liked to sit in the back with sleeping bags and blankets so that we could look up at the sky and see the stars just like our boys did! We enjoyed seeing an occasional falling star.

Our Generous Neighbors

One of our golfing friends built a home which was a mansion compared to our little cabin. It was right near the edge of the cliff where the boys had built their tree house years before.

They let Mike use their Jeep when they weren't there, and he could drive it around Wawona. When their grandparents came up, he took them riding all around our little community. They really enjoyed that! Our friends also would drive up in their Cadillac convertible to their *cabin.* They let our son Don take it one night to Bass Lake where teenagers went to dance at "The Falls."

We couldn't get over how generous they were, and the boys always took care with the responsibility and trust they had in them. We watched over their place when they didn't come up, even though they had a caretaker come by once in awhile.

A Hike in the High Country

Yosemite had High Camps where one could stay overnight or longer in tents, with meals included. Our whole family went on these trips at different times.

We'd park our car in the parking lot at Tuolumne. That was the base camp before heading up to the other high camps. It had tents for sleeping and a big tent for eating. We were told not to leave any food in the car and also not to leave any windows open at all. That's why we saw all the broken glass on the parking lot.

The bears were very smart; they could put their claws in a barely open window and pull on the windows and break them. That explained all the broken glass we saw. Especially, if food had been left in the cars.

They'd also scratch the cars crawling all over them looking for food. We made sure that our windows were closed and no trace of food left inside so they wouldn't bother our car.

There were seven High Camps in all. (We eventually went to all of them several times.) There was one hazardous trip in particular, but I'll come back to that later. Some trails were straight up where we had to switch back and forth. Most camps were seven to eight mile trips; one camp was twelve; and one was just one mile. They were all worth the journey.

Mike, his friend, and our hiking friends went on this trip. Keith and Don couldn't make it as they had other commitments. Mike asked his dad and me if he and his friend could go on ahead and take a little shortcut instead of following the trail. His dad said it was all right, but I wasn't happy about the arrangement. I feared they might get lost or meet up with bears, but it turned out fine because we could see them in the distance.

His dad said he had faith in them, because they'd had a lot of experience hiking all around Yosemite and elsewhere in the mountains. As it turned out, they were waiting for us when we got to the camp site.

When we arrived, we checked in at a large tent with a cement floor. Ice cold lemonade was served right away, and after such a long, arduous hike, the lemonade was so refreshing. We were assigned our tent which had a cement floor, a little wood stove, and four little beds.

We were delighted to have the wood stove because the nights got extremely cold in the high altitude. The shower facilities were on a first-come, first-served basis. The showers were canvas-framed, with water heated by the sun. We all took showers and the warm water felt so good on our aching muscles; then everyone took a short nap.

Dinner time was announced by clanging on a metal triangle that echoed all over the mountain. The family-style dinner was served in the big tent. All the foodstuff had been brought up on pack mules.

The meal prepared for us was delicious. A husband and wife and college kids were in charge of the High Camp. After dinner, a campfire was lit outside, and the young student-workers entertained us with music and songs.

On this particular night, a young man played the guitar and we sang along with him. After a while, we were pretty tired and decided to go back to our tent. Since our tent had four small beds in it, Mike and his friend put their sleeping bags on a rug on the floor at the foot of our beds.

This Awful Noise

During the night, we heard an awful noise that awakened everyone except for my husband who slept right on through. We figured it was a bear prowling around outside.

Now that I was awake, I needed to visit the outhouse, and Mike said he would go with me. We took a flash light with us. We were both a little leery about going out in the pitch-black night, and maybe seeing a bear out there.

We went very slowly, flashing our light all around to see if there was anything around. When we got to the outhouse, Mike waited outside. He called out that he thought he saw the bear. I was just starting to open the door to come out when Mike ran inside and said, "Sorry Mom, but I think I just saw the bear out there."

We didn't know what to do and were so scared! Stuck inside the outhouse, we waited, listening for noises outside. After a while since we didn't hear anything, I opened the door a little and tried to look out. It was so dark that we couldn't see a thing. I was afraid to turn the flashlight on, afraid of seeing the bear. Finally I flashed the light all around but didn't see anything that looked like a bear.

That's when we made a mad dash to our tent. When we got inside I went right for my husband's bed; he was awake now. Mike got into my bed, and his friend took Mike's sleeping bag and put it under his sleeping bag. It was like playing musical chairs with beds.

We decided the horrible noise we heard was the huge bear that we were pretty sure we saw, and that it finally went on his way. It took a while for all of us to get back to sleep. The next morning at breakfast, all the other hikers were talking about the awful noise they also heard during the night. They too, thought it was a bear hunting for food or looking for a mate. We told them of our experience and of Mike and me seeing the bear.

A Short Cut

After a nice leisurely breakfast, we bid the other hikers goodbye and went back to our tent to pack and leave. While we were having breakfast that morning, one of the young girls serving us asked which camp we were going to next.

We told her, and she mentioned that there was a shorter way of going instead of following the longer trail. She and her fellow workers went that way to visit each other during their time off, and said that it would cut off a mile or two. She explained how to find the way to my husband.

I was a little skeptical about going on without a trail, but our friends, Mike and his friend all agreed to try it. Part of the way was on solid granite rock and most of it was downhill. I was really glad when we finally got back on the trail.

We saw many lovely wild flowers. On the way down, we saw a sign that said "Babcock Lake 3 miles." All of us agreed it would surely be nice to take a dip in the lake. It was such a warm beautiful day and only three miles out of our way.

When we reached the lake, we were impressed

with the huge granite boulders around it. We really had to climb over each one to get to the lake. While climbing over them, we saw a couple of snakes crawling around and some cute little marmots. We finally reached the water and took our boots off, but went in with our shorts and T-shirts. It felt really good as we were quite hot by then. By the time we hiked back down the main path, our clothes were dry. It was a highly enjoyable experience for all of us, and we planned to do it again the next summer with another high camp.

Another High Country Trip

When we returned to our car, we saw a lot of broken glass on the asphalt, but our car had not been disturbed. We were happy that the bears hadn't done any damage to our car.

My husband and I planned another High Country trip with our friends. It was just the four of us this time. We hiked up to 10,000 foot altitude of switch-back trails. Again it was a seven or eight mile hike with the only way up to these Camps either by hiking or riding mules.

A cowboy and his horse, with his three or four mules behind, brought up all the supplies for the camps. Sometimes there would be people who did not like to hike but rode the mules. On this particular trip, we saw a dreadful sight of two dead mules over the side and wondered how that had happened.

My husband and my friend's husband took turns carrying quite a big backpack. The pack contained everything the four of us would need: a change of clothes for our stay at the camp, some food such as cheese and crackers, cookies, fruit, and a bottle of wine to have before dinner.

As before, when we arrived, we were given a glass of ice cold lemonade, which we were happy to get after the hard hike. We were assigned a tent with a wood stove as it gets very cold up in the high altitude. We were lucky again to get a tent with four beds so that we could be together. After our much-appreciated showers we took a short nap. It was the same routine more or less every time.

After the much-needed nap, we sat outside by a stream with a view of the mountains, and had our glass of wine in the beautiful surroundings. The camp again served a wonderful dinner, and we lingered talking to the other hikers.

Then we all went outside to sit by the camp fire. We were entertained again by a young man playing the guitar, and all of us sang along with him. It was all so relaxing and enjoyable sitting around the camp fire that we stayed longer than we intended.

We got up early the next day and started packing for our trip down, looking forward to the wonderful breakfast, and visiting with our fellow travelers. Then after breakfast, we went on to hike down those seven or eight miles.

A Harrowing Experience

We were on the trail for a couple of miles when we heard and then saw the cowboy coming down the switch-back above us, followed by three mules attached to him by a lead rope. We immediately tried to get out of his way as the path was so narrow, and over the side was about a five hundred foot drop off. I've always been afraid of horses (mules) so was afraid to get too close to them.

It was impossible to get out of his way. If we went one way, it was straight up the embankment; the other way was straight down over the side. He stopped just before he reached us, and asked us if we wanted to ride on one of his mules. He said it would help him control them instead of leading three of them down unburdened.

Our husbands told my friend and me to get on the mules and they would walk behind us. They said it would save us from hiking down. I really didn't want to, but my friend thought it would be a nice experience for us although I was beginning to think that this venture was foolhardy.

I put on a brave face and proceeded to climb up

on the last mule, all the while my heart was beating fast! The cowboy unfastened the rope and told me how to hold the reins. He said to hold the reins loosely in each palm, and not to wrap them around my hands. If by chance the mule spooked, I could be dragged with my hands tangled in the reins.

Well, that's all I needed to hear to scare me and I wanted to get off. I looked over at my friend, and she looked rather confident, so we started down the trail. In just a few minutes my mule had other ideas and started to go really fast up the steep embankment.

I had a hard time trying to stay on the mule. I thought I would fall off backwards because the embankment was very steep. I didn't know what to do so I yelled to the cowboy, "What do I do?" He called back "Pull on the reins!" I did, and the mule finally came back down.

We were way in back, and my husband was so far back we couldn't see each other. Then my mule decided to take off down a treacherous, narrow trail going so very fast, and so close to the edge that he shoved the other mules and the cowboy, passing them. I couldn't see how my mule stayed on the trail.

By then I had my eyes closed and my heart was pounding with fear. I tried to control my breathing but when I finally opened my eyes, I thought my life was over! I was going to end up where we had seen the two dead mules down below. I tried to call back to the cowboy, but he was busy holding on to the other mule. My mule had spooked his mule and he was acting up, too.

I couldn't see my husband; he was so far back and didn't know what was happening. In the meantime my mule was still running close to the dangerous edge and I was thinking, "We're going over the side! How am I going to get off him?" I knew I had to do something quick!

I kept visualizing those two dead mules at the bottom of the canyon. It was now or never! I let go of the reins and proceeded to slip off him. It felt as if I were doing this all in slow motion, but I hit the ground hard, right on the edge of the cliff, and was afraid to move. I was shaking all over!

I looked up to see my mule go over the side and plunge over the heavily vegetated cliff. He tumbled and rolled quite a ways, but by a miracle was caught in some shrubbery on his back, which stopped his falling all the way down. He was squirming around trying to get back on his feet, and he finally got up.

It took a while for the cowboy to coax him back on to the trail, encouraging him all the way. The mule finally made it back up. The cowboy took hold of his reins and checked him over to see that he was all right. He tied him on next to him and his horse.

My husband and my friends came running to get me as I hadn't moved. I was still shaking with fear. My husband helped me up; my legs were so wobbly I could hardly stand on them. I said, "I never want to get on another horse or mule again." The cowboy came to see if I was all right and said, "They know when someone is nervous or scared which tends to spook them."

I certainly was scared; actually I was terrified. By the time I was ready to resume our hike down, it took time for me to settle down. I was so euphoric to be back hiking on the trail again and that I was fine. The cowboy I assumed was happy his mules were safe.

It took some time for me to get over the threatening situation, and enduring the harrowing experience of almost going over the edge. I've always enjoyed hiking in the high country and continued to do so, but never again on a mule.

I did get on a horse again a few years later. It was on a beautiful breakfast ride on flat country, and the horse they picked for me was so docile I enjoyed the ride this time.

Our Brand New Van

One summer my friend and I decided to go hiking by ourselves when our husbands couldn't make it. We had just bought a brand new van that my husband had paneled inside and special- ordered a queen size bed for it.

The van had carpeting and a nice little ice box. It was for our short camping trips. My friend and I took it up to the camp ground in Tuolumne so we could go on different hikes. Our camp site was quite small. In order to park my van, I had to squeeze between two small pine trees.

That evening, we heated a noodle casserole for dinner. After we were through eating, we cleaned up what we used. A young man came by and to tell everyone that someone had sighted a bear and that we had better not leave any food around that the bear could get to.

When we were through with washing the pan and dishes, we threw the water out near us thinking that was all right. After hearing about the bear, we got down on our hands and knees with a flashlight to see if there was any food that had been thrown out with the dish water. We were satisfied that we had cleaned it all up and went inside the van.

We started talking about the bear and decided we had to leave a window open just a little for some air. So we put a small carpet on the window in case the bear put his claws on it and pulled it down. We knew the window would shatter if he did that. We were really scared! We finally went to sleep and luckily nothing happened.

We went on two different hikes of seven and six miles in the two days we were there. The last day we hiked, we were way up when a thunder and lightning storm came and a hard rain began, I remembered that I had left the windows on the van down and I worried the rain would get into the van.

We were also scared of lightning hitting the trees we were under. So my friend and I literally ran down the trail those six miles to get to our van. We watched out for the lightning as we ran. When we got down, everything was fine. We got in the van and I proceeded to back out between the two pine trees. It was such a tight squeeze; I had a hard time and I scratched both sides of my new van. I felt terrible! When we got back, I told my husband that the trees must have *swollen* because of all the rain! He couldn't believe I said that!

Snakes...Ugh!

One afternoon as Keith, Don, and their Dad were riding down the dirt road to the cabin, they heard a rattlesnake and then saw it crawling under a log. Dad parked the car by the cabin and then went down to the shed to get a rake. He went back up to the log under which the snake had crawled and found it. The rattlesnake was a little more than three feet long.

The boys' Dad killed it as he was afraid that it would harm them or the other families who had cabins nearby. We learned there was a sawmill there in Wawona owned by the man from whom we bought our property. There was a lot of sawdust there from previous sawmills, and that was where the rattlesnakes hibernated. Previously, our neighbors had killed a couple of rattlesnakes, but this was the only one we ever saw and we were glad of that!

I did come across a snake curled right where I stepped up to the driver's side of our truck. I was on my way to play golf one morning and, as usual, was in a hurry. I didn't see it at first, but when I started to step up on the running board, there it was curled! His color was just like the ground so no wonder I hadn't noticed it. It scared me because I thought it was another rattlesnake! Then I realized it was a harmless gopher snake. I guess I scared it, because it crawled away very fast.

Hunting Season

Since our family came up on all the holidays, summer vacations, and weekends, my husband decided to just bring the men who worked for him up to our cabin during the fall hunting season. They mentioned how they liked to hunt, but my husband was not a hunter. He just couldn't see killing any animal.

He invited them to stay at our cabin and hunt outside of Yosemite. They played a game of golf when they first got there, and were amazed at how many deer they saw on the course. My husband explained that during hunting season most of the deer came inside the park. It was odd how the animals knew when to come, too!

Early the next morning, the men got up and left to hunt in the forest outside the park. They were gone all day and returned late. They claimed they hadn't seen one buck all day. My husband made a rock fire pit in the yard, and had a good fire going when they got back. He had chairs around where they could sit and relax after their long day.

While they were telling their stories, a beautiful

buck came quietly up behind them. My husband knew it must be *Bambi*, and told the men to look around slowly and there he was in full splendor with his big antlers. He was such a beautiful looking buck that the men were in awe as he sauntered right up next to them. They couldn't believe that they had been out all day looking for a buck to shoot and here was this one right next to them being so friendly.

One of the men said, "Quick get my gun." Of course he was kidding; my husband would never let them shoot here in Yosemite and certainly not our dear *Bambi*! He then told the story of how *Bambi* had come into our lives. *Bambi* stayed around for quite a while and even came up to one of the men to take a drink out of his glass as if he were one of them. The men still couldn't believe what they were seeing. *Bambi* finally left and went over the side down to the river.

The Flooding

I wrote earlier that our swimming hole over the side of the cliff wasn't there anymore because of a flood that took place one Christmas holiday and diverted the river.

Mike and I had come up a week ahead of the rest of the family. Keith and Don, now working with their Dad for the same power company, came up with him. While Mike and I were at the cabin, it rained steadily all week. The river current was so strong and rose so high we could hear the boulders hitting each other. It shook our cabin like an earthquake. The water changed the course of the river by us and that's why we no longer had our swimming hole. The river by the bridge where the boys liked to swim was almost up to the bridge.

Yosemite Valley was flooded with high watermarks in the houses. When my husband and I visited the Park Superintendent's house, he showed us the water mark. They had a difficult time cleaning out the mud. We were glad our little cabin was on high ground. Nothing leaked because we built it very sturdily.

Mike's Different Jobs

When my husband was building our cabin, and putting in the wiring, our sons had watched their Dad, and became quite good at it, too.

The Ranger in Wawona heard how the boys had helped their Dad with the wiring and asked Mike if he would help him wire the house he was building in Oakhurst for his retirement. Mike told him he would enjoy working with him, and use all his knowledge in building the house.

Since his brothers were at home with their Dad, Mike had his good friend with whom to pal around. They both put their applications in, and went to work for the *Yosemite Park and Curry Co.,* working at the gas station in Wawona. They were called, "S.O.B's" which stood for "Standard Oil Boys." They really enjoyed that job. On their days off, they would still go hiking and swimming, and get in a little mischief now and then!

One day I was across the river getting my hair done by a woman whose husband worked for the park service. A car drove by going quite fast around the curve in front of her cabin. She ran to the window and said, "If I find out who's driving that car, I'm going to report him!" I also looked, and was surprised to see it was Mike, driving his Volkswagen. I didn't let on that it was my son driving; I was too embarrassed to admit it was my son. Mike was on his way to pick up his friend.

Later, when Mike and his friend came to our cabin, I told him what happened, and said, "You better drive slower from now on or you'll get a ticket, the lady knows your car." He said he would drive slower from now on as he didn't want to get a ticket.

When Mike and his friend met some of our friends for the first time, they thought his friend was my son as both he and I had black hair. The friend's mother had red hair and they thought Mike, a redhead, was her son. The boys whimsically never let on the difference. The two of them had some good times, and have remained good friends to this day.

Making a Movie

A movie was made while we were there called, "36 Hours," transforming Wawona into the Black Forest of Bavaria. The park dump became part of the forest and the bears would quite often get in the way of filming. The film makers would wait so as not to disturb the bears as they were scavenging for food. Sometimes the bears would even watch them while the filming was in progress.

The Wawona Hotel was turned into an Allied Military Hospital. A sign was stretched across the front of the hotel reading, "The United States Military Hospital." It sometimes distracted people who were looking to stay at the Hotel. James Garner and Rod Taylor were the main actors, and while they weren't working, played a lot of golf. It was a company of such great proportions that we wondered how they managed it all.

Our wonderful Friends

Our little cabin had just three rooms and a loft, but we had wonderful dinner parties with all our friends. One party that I remember especially well was our 25th wedding anniversary. We invited all our friends in Yosemite which was quite a few people.

The party was catered by the chef of the Ahwahnee Hotel, one of our golfing friends. We set up long tables with white table cloths in our driveway to accommodate all our friends who presented us with a money tree of 25 silver dollars and many lovely gifts.

Mike and his friend parked all the cars in whatever space they could find. When it came time to pay the chef, he said, "This is on me!" My husband and I were overwhelmed at his generosity. He was a wonderful friend, a good golfer, and an excellent chef!

This little cabin was such a major part of our lives, and what a wonderful life we all had in Yosemite. Our boys still go up to Wawona, and once in a while we go up too, but now they *rent the* cabins, and *play* golf, swim and still hike, and reminisce about their youth there.

But our cabin is long gone, and in its place is a two story cabin, and next to it is our friends' little cabin. My one regret is that we sold our cabin. At the time, we thought we didn't want to put up with frozen pipes, power outages, and to go through snow past our knees anymore. But as we look back, now we would gladly go through it all again!

There aren't many bears around now; they seem to stay up in the high country. There are still many deer, but no one has seen Bambi. We hope that he is living the good life, and not in some hunter's sight. And yes, the boys still honk their horns as they pass that certain area in Fish Camp!

ABOUT THE AUTHOR:

Sophia Kaeser and her husband, Keith, with their three sons, Keith, Don, and Mike owned a cabin in Wawona, Yosemite National Park for twenty years. They spent the major part of those twenty years at their little cabin. It was their life and the family did everything together. They skied, hiked, and played golf. They had wonderful dinners and cocktail parties. They also made so many wonderful friends, both people and animals. Her first book was *Our Family Adventures with Bears.* Now retired and living in Temecula, California, they still occasionally visit Wawona, Yosemite with their children. Sophia and Keith have eleven grandchildren and eighteen great-grandchildren. The boys and their families rent cabins now and visit several times a year. Now they **play** golf *on the same course, and still hike and swim in the same rivers.*